# KINGDOMBUILDERS:
# UNLEASHING YOUR POWER TO IMPACT THE WORLD

Discover Your Divine Purpose, Overcome Challenges, and Change the World!

## KIBAMBA NIMON

Published in Canada by Kibamba Nimon

Author : Kibamba Nimon

Illustrations: Canva

*Unless otherwise indicated, biblical verses and names are cited from the Amplified Bible and the International Children's Bible*

© 2024

ISBN: 978-2-9823085-1-0

# CONTENTS

**Foreword . . . . . . . . . . . . . . . . . . . . . . . . . . . . . . . . 5**

01. Encountering the King - Discovering
    Your Divine Sovereign . . . . . . . . . . . . . . . . . . . . . 8

02. Embracing your kingdom identity . . . . . . . . . . . . . 13

03. Unveiling Your Kingdom Purpose . . . . . . . . . . . . 17

04. Facing the Giants . . . . . . . . . . . . . . . . . . . . . . . 26

05. Conquering the Flesh . . . . . . . . . . . . . . . . . . . . 36
    Understanding the Internal Struggles . . . . . . . . . . 37

06. Navigating Friendship and Peer Pressure . . . . . . . . 41
    The Influence of the World . . . . . . . . . . . . . . . . . 42

07. Overcoming the Weapon of Fear . . . . . . . . . . . . . 45
    Unmasking the Tactics of the Devil . . . . . . . . . . . 46

**Activity - Operation Giant Slayer: Your Mission Begins . . . . 49**

08. Deepening Connections through Prayer
    and Spiritual Discipline . . . . . . . . . . . . . . . . . . . 53
    The Power of Intentional Connection . . . . . . . . . . 54

09. Empowered to Impact . . . . . . . . . . . . . . . . . . . . 57
    Unleashing Your Kingdom Influence . . . . . . . . . . 58

*I write to you, young men, because you are strong; the word of God lives in you, and you have defeated the Evil One.*
**1 john 2:14**

# FOREWORD

My dear Friend,

I am happy you picked this book. I wrote it to share with you some practical tools based on the Word of God to help you go through life without fear and with great courage.

There are lot of things going on in the world you are growing in today. I am sure there are many questions you are asking yourself and your brilliant mind is eager to discover the truth.

Through this book, you will discover who you really are and what you are meant to do in this world. You are not too young to start thinking about that. There was once a young man about your age who was given a great mission to save an entire kingdom. The kingdom was going to be destroyed because of the wickedness of the leaders and its people. He was sent to warn them and invite them to turn away from the wrong path. He got scared by the assignment because of his young age and his reply was "I am too young! I cannot speak in public". But little did he know that he was born for that purpose and all he needed to do was to trust in the one who called him and equipped him for that specific assignment.

You too, you have a great assignment awaiting you to be discovered and fulfilled. But to be successful, you need to understand one important truth: Jesus Christ is the beginning and the end goal of your mission. Everything starts with him and ends with him. John, one of his closest friends wrote this about him:

---

*IN THE beginning [before all time] was the Word (Christ), and the Word was with God, and the Word was God Himself. He was present originally with God. All things were made and came into existence through Him; and without Him was not even one thing made that has come into being.*
**(John 1:1-3 Amplified Bible)**

In these first sentences of his message, john explains that Jesus is the Word, and it is only through him that everything that you see was created: the trees, the mountains, the oceans, the animals, people and so much more. Before anything has ever existed, Jesus was there ! Is this not wonderful? It also means that, before you came into this world, Jesus knew you and everything about you.

John then goes on to write:

---

*In Him was Life, and the Life was the Light of men. And the Light shines on in the darkness, for the darkness has never overpowered it [put it out or absorbed it].*
**(John 1:4-5 Amplified Bible)**

So, Jesus is not only The Word, but he also carries inside him Life and Light. The beauty of light is that it chases away darkness. Have you ever experienced being uncomfortable in a place at home, school or anywhere else, just because it was dark? You might have felt fear, and I am sure you wanted to get out of there quickly. The reason you felt that way is because when it's dark you can't see much, and you don't know what is going on around you. It makes you feel powerless. But the good news is that Jesus is the Life and Light that we need to walk through a very dark world.

Through his message, John points out the number one resource that you need to be successful in your assignment:

*The Light – Jesus. Without Him, it will be mission impossible but with Him, all things are possible.*

# CHAPTER 1

## ENCOUNTERING THE KING - DISCOVERING YOUR DIVINE SOVEREIGN

**D**id you know that the kingdom of God is the message Jesus proclaimed from the start to the end of his mission on the earth? The kingdom of God is also the message he instructed his disciples (those who follow him) to proclaim as well. It is the topic he told them to pray about and it is what he commended to seek more than anything else in this life.

What is a kingdom you might ask? A kingdom is a territory or a domain or a place where a king lives and rules. Apart of the king, you also have people. It won't make any sense if it was just one person living there, right? So, it takes people, inhabitants, citizens, a domain, and a king to make a kingdom. In a kingdom you have rules, rights, and duties. You can recognize the citizens by the way they talk, dress up and carry themselves around.

So, if Jesus spent all his time teaching about the kingdom of God you must understand these important truths:

- God is a King who rules and reigns over His people living in His domain.
- When you accept to follow Jesus, you become a child of God which makes you a child of the King. You are royalty !
- You have great privileges as a child of the King and citizen of the kingdom, but you also must live by the rules set by the King.

The central figure in a kingdom is the king. In most of the stories of princesses or knights you might have heard of, I am sure the king is described as a majestic figure who wears the most beautiful, shimmering robes and who has on his head a crown glistened with precious gems. This is the picture that comes to our mind when we think of the greatness of a king. But what truly makes a king glorious is not just his fancy attire or his magnificent castle. It's the way he rules his kingdom.

Jesus, known as a great storyteller, told a story to help people understand who God really is and what kind of King He is. The story was about a father and his two sons. He told this story because the religious leaders, people who claimed to know God better than everyone else, were complaining that he, Jesus, was associating and eating with sinners (people who were living their lives outside of the will of God – the "not so good people").

The story was reported for us by another friend of Jesus by the name of Luke (15:11-32 Amplified Bible ). Let's dive into it !

---

*"There was a man who had two sons. The younger son spoke to his father. He said, 'Father, give me my share of the family property.' So, the father divided his property between his two sons.*

---

The first thing I want you to understand is that in the Jewish culture, back then and even today, a child can only inherit, have his share of the family possessions when his father is no longer alive. With that in mind, if we rephrase the request of the younger son, this would be what he said to his father : **"I wish you were dead. I don't want anything to do with you. I don't want any part in the family legacy. I just want my stuff. Give me my share of the goods now, as if you were already dead"**. His attitude was very shocking and devastating. Yet, the father did give him his share.

The story continues like this,

---

*"Not long after that, the younger son packed up all he had. Then he left for a country far away. There he wasted his money on wild living. He spent everything he had. Then the*

*whole country ran low on food. So, the son didn't have what he needed. He went to work for someone who lived in that country. That person sent the son to the fields to feed the pigs. 16 The son wanted to fill his stomach with the food the pigs were eating. But no one gave him anything.*

The very next thing the younger son did after collecting his share was to move away from his family to a far distant place. It is obvious he no longer wanted to have any relationship with his father, and he had no appreciation for what was given which he totally wasted. But when his adventure took a very sad turn, he got all his senses back:

*"Then he began to think clearly again. He said, 'How many of my father's hired servants have more than enough food! But here I am dying from hunger! I will get up and go back to my father. I will say to him, "Father, I have sinned against heaven. And I have sinned against you. I am no longer fit to be called your son. Make me like one of your hired servants."? So, he got up and went to his father.*
*While the son was still a long way off, his father saw him. He was filled with tender love for his son. He ran to him. He threw his arms around him and kissed him.*
*"The son said to him, 'Father, I have sinned against heaven and against you. I am no longer fit to be called your son.'*
*"But the father said to his servants, 'Quick! Bring the best robe and put it on him. Put a ring on his finger and sandals on his feet. Bring the fattest calf and kill it. Let's have a feast and celebrate. This son of mine was dead. And now he is alive again. He was lost. And now he is found.' So, they began to celebrate.*

The attitude of the father demonstrates great love and compassion towards his younger son who did not deserve it. He gave his son every right back as if he had never walked out on him in an outrageous way. Regardless of what his son did, the father wiped everything away in one moment when he expressed his joy to see him back again.

The story does not end there but let us pause here and reflect on what we can learn about the kind of King God is. The father in the story is the figure of God. The first thing I want to underline from the story is that God as King wants to have a close relationship with all His children. He is not a far distant god who does not have any interest in the lives of those who worship him, meaning people who willingly follow his laws and rules. Yet, he allows us to reject Him.

*But Anyone who rejects God wastes their gifts and resources just like the younger son.*

The second thing I want you to notice is that God rules with love and great compassion. The father in this story had every reason to be very angry and mad at the younger son. I don't think anyone would blame him if he had turned his back on his son when he returned to him. Yet, he ran to him with great joy and did not stop kissing him because he sincerely was more than happy to see his son back again. Towards his son, the father has expressed mercy (did not punish him even though he deserved to be punished) and grace (gave him what he did not deserve).

*And this is how God, the King, rules His Kingdom: He rules with mercy and grace. He rules with LOVE.*

# CHAPTER 2

**EMBRACING YOUR KINGDOM IDENTITY.**

## Imagine this!

A young man needed to go on a long journey. That trip was very costly and required he spent all he had to purchase the train ticket that would take him to his destination. He had no money left to spend on anything else after purchasing the ticket. Once on the train, even though he was hungry, each time the steward would bring him food he would refuse to have any. So, he traveled for days with an empty stomach. When he arrived at his destination, one of the stewards asked him why he did not want to have any food. To that question, he replied he had no money to pay for food. The steward then told him that the food was included in his ticket, and therefore he did not have to pay anything extra.

What would be your reaction if it was you? I bet you would certainly be very disappointed in yourself. This is the consequence of ignorance. Imagine how much this young fellow would have enjoyed his journey had he known all he had access to with his train ticket. Not knowing what you have rightfully been given to live this life triumphantly will lead you to disappointment and unfulfillment. But the best way to avoid this is to get to know your identity as a child of the King and fully embrace it.

Let's get back to the tale of the father and his two sons that we started in the last chapter. When the younger son came back home apologising for what he did, his father yelled 3 orders to the servants in his house. First, he ordered them to bring the finest robe which signifies dignity. In other words, the robe gives him the value, the honor, the respect attached to his statue as the son of the family. His former shameful behavior is completely covered and not to be mentioned again.

The second thing the father asked the servant to bring was a ring. Imagine a special ring that's more than just jewelry—it's like a tiny, personal stamp that tells a story. A signet ring is a ring with a special design or symbol carved into the surface. This design is unique to the person wearing it, like their own secret code.

Back in ancient times, people used signet rings to seal important documents or letters. They would press the ring into hot wax, leaving behind the design as a mark of authenticity. It was like saying, 'This letter is from me, and it's important. Today, signet rings are still used as symbols of identity and belonging. Some families have their own signet rings that get passed down through generations, each one carrying the history and values of the family. So, when you see someone wearing a signet ring, remember that it's not just a piece of jewelry—it's a connection to their past, their family, and their own unique story.

By putting a ring on his son's finger, the father was giving him back full family membership and authority. He could act on behalf of the family without any problem.

The last order the father gave was to bring his son sandals for his feet. Back in those days, only servants and slaves went barefoot. The sandals represent his worth as a son, not a slave. He would not have to work to sustain himself or pay back his debt in any way. He was completely forgiven.

*Like the younger son, we reject God too when we choose to live life on our own without Him. We put distance and cut the relationship. We always end up wasting a lot and find ourselves in difficult situations.*

When we choose to return to him, just like the younger son in the story, he always takes us back. The father in the story ran to his son even though in that culture it was not acceptable for a man of his social status to run in public. It was considered a disgrace, a shame. By going against the culture, the father took the shame off of his son and placed it on himself.

*Jesus Christ did the same for you and I when he took our sin and shame no matter how great and placed it on himself and paid the penalty for it on the cross.*

So, when you place your faith in Jesus, your relationship with God the King is immediately restored. As a child of God, you are given a dignified robe, authority to act on behalf of the King and His kingdom, and you are promised an endless inheritance.

*This my friend is who you are !*

# CHAPTER 3

## UNVEILING YOUR KINGDOM PURPOSE

In the grand tapestry of the Kingdom of God, each thread has a purpose—a calling that intertwines with the divine design. The idea of purpose can be both exciting and puzzling. What does it mean to have a purpose, and how do you uncover your God given purpose?

*purpose is the reason for which something is done or created or for which something exists.*

According to the Oxford languages dictionary, purpose is the reason for which something is done or created or for which something exists. For example, the purpose of a car is to help you commute from point A to point B faster than a bicycle or a horse or by foot and in a more comfortable condition.

Remember the young boy I told you about in the introduction of the book, who was afraid of his assignment because of his age? He was a great man of God back in ancient Israel time. His name was Jeremiah. When God came to him, this is what He told him:

*Before I made you in your mother's womb, I chose you. Before you were born, I set you apart for a special work. I appointed you as a prophet to the nations."*
**(Jeremiah 1:5 ICB)**

In the same manner, understand that you also exist for a very specific work that God has prepared for you to do before you were even born. You have a purpose. Now, your purpose is not a distant mystery but a story that is already inside of you waiting to unfold. It's the unique melody only you can play in the symphony of God's creation.

To help you grasp this truth I invite you to dive into the stories of Kingdom heroes—ordinary people who discovered their extraordinary callings and lived purposeful despite the many challenges they faced.

## "Dorcas: A Testament of Faith and Compassion"

Step back in time to ancient Jerusalem and meet Dorcas, a remarkable woman whose story transcends the pages of history. Found in the Bible, in the book of Acts (chapter 9:36-42), Dorcas's tale begins in the bustling city of Joppa, where her acts of faith and compassion left an indelible mark on those around her.

Dorcas was known for her unwavering dedication to helping others. She spent her days sewing garments for the needy, tirelessly working to provide clothing for widows and the less fortunate in her community. In a time when women's contributions were often overlooked, Dorcas stood out as a beacon of kindness and generosity.

But Dorcas's story takes a miraculous turn when tragedy strikes. She falls ill and passes away, leaving her friends and fellow believers grief-stricken. Yet, in the midst of their sorrow, they refuse to give up hope. They send for Peter, one of Jesus's friends, believing that he can bring about a miracle.

And indeed, Peter arrives and performs a miracle beyond imagination. With a prayer and a touch, he raises Dorcas from the dead, restoring her to life and bringing joy and wonder to all who witness it. Dorcas's resurrection becomes a powerful testament to the faith and compassion that defined her life.

Dorcas's story isn't just a tale from ancient times—it's a timeless example of faith in action. Her selfless acts of kindness and her unwavering devotion to serving others serve as an inspiration to people of all ages, reminding us of the power of compassion to transform lives and bring hope to those in need.

## "Courage in the Shadows: The Unforgettable Story of Corrie ten Boom"

Meet Corrie ten Boom ! Amid World War II, while the world was engulfed in chaos and fear, Corrie and her family stood tall against the darkness of the Nazi regime.

But wait, let's back up a bit. World War II was a huge, history-shaping conflict that engulfed the entire globe. It pitted countries against each other in a battle for freedom and justice. At the center of it all were the Nazis, a group of ruthless rulers in Germany led by the infamous Adolf Hitler. These guys were bad news—they believed in a twisted ideology of hate and superiority, and they didn't hesitate to unleash their terror on anyone who stood in their way.

One of the most horrifying aspects of the Nazi regime was the Holocaust. This was a systematic attempt to exterminate millions of innocent people, primarily Jews, along with others who were deemed "undesirable" by the Nazis. It was a dark chapter in human history, marked by unimaginable suffering and loss.

Now, imagine being caught in the middle of all this chaos. That's where Corrie ten Boom and her family found themselves. But instead of cowering in fear, they bravely chose to fight back. They transformed their home into a secret haven, hiding Jews from the clutches of the enemy. Can you imagine the excitement and danger of living in a house filled with hidden rooms and secret passageways?

But the stakes were high, and eventually, the ten Boom family was discovered and captured by the Nazis. They were sent to brutal concentration camps, where they endured unimaginable hardships and suffering. Yet, even in the darkest of places, Corrie's spirit remained unbroken. She spread light and hope wherever she went after being released from the concentration camp, showing that even in the bleakest of times, courage and kindness shine brightest.

Corrie ten Boom's story isn't just about history—it's about finding the hero within yourself! Through her life you learn that courage isn't about being fearless, but about standing tall even when you're shaking in your boots. She once said, **" Faith sees the invisible, believes the unbelievable, and receives the impossible**."

## "Nick Vujicic: Embracing Life's Extraordinary Journey"

Now let's step into the remarkable life of Nick Vujicic, a modern-day hero who has overcome incredible challenges with unwavering courage and a boundless spirit! Born without arms and legs due to a rare condition called tetra-amelia syndrome, Nick faced hurdles that most people couldn't even fathom. But instead of letting his physical limitations define him, Nick turned them into stepping stones for an extraordinary journey filled with triumph, inspiration, and hope.

Nick's journey began with his birth, an event that defied all expectations. Tetra-amelia syndrome is a congenital disorder characterized by the absence of all four limbs. Imagine entering the world without arms to reach out for a hug or legs to take your first steps. It's a daunting reality, but Nick refused to let it hold him back. From a young age, he learned to adapt and innovate, using his mouth to do tasks that others took for granted.

Growing up presented its own set of challenges for Nick. He faced relentless bullying and discrimination, with peers often mocking him and excluding him because of his differences. This kind of social rejection can be incredibly painful and isolating, but Nick didn't let it break his spirit. Instead, he chose to rise above the negativity, finding strength in his faith and the support of his family and friends.

Despite the obstacles he faced, Nick remained determined to live life to the fullest. He pursued his education, earning a degree in accounting and financial planning. He learned to surf, play golf, and even skydive, proving that with determination and creativity, anything is possible.

As Nick's fame grew, so did his platform for spreading positivity and encouragement. Through his motivational speeches, bestselling books, and uplifting messages, he has inspired millions of people around the world to embrace their uniqueness and pursue their dreams with passion and purpose.

*faithpot.com*
*Nick around 8 years old*

Nick Vujicic's story isn't just about overcoming physical challenges—it's about embracing life's journey with courage, resilience, and unwavering faith. He is a living proof that we can truly do all things through Christ who gives us strength.

What makes Dorcas, Corrie, and Nick extraordinary? It's not just their talents, or abilities or even their material possession but rather their willingness to align all they have with the purposes of the Kingdom: take care of the needy, stand for what is right, spread the good news of the love of God. Their callings weren't dictated by societal expectations or fleeting desires; they were shaped by a deeper understanding of who they were in God's Kingdom.

It's very important for you to understand that:

***God has made us what we are. In Christ Jesus, God made us new people so that we would do good works. God had planned in advance those good works for us. He had planned for us to live our lives doing them***
*(Ephesian 2:10 ICB)*

*You are the King's masterpiece!*

God indeed carefully designed you with purpose he hid inside of you. Your first mission is to find it and then fulfill it. To help you find it, turn to the next page to discover your first gadget – The Gift Compass !

# TOOLS FOR UNVEILING YOUR PURPOSE

Now, as you embark on the journey of discovering your unique purpose, let's introduce you to a powerful tool—the Gift Compass. Imagine a compass that doesn't point north but directs you toward the unique gifts and talents God has woven into the fabric of your being. Follow the steps below to find out where the compass will lead you:

### Step 1. Prayer

The first direction the compass will point you to is to engage in prayer, asking God for guidance in unveiling your purpose. Jesus Himself encourages us to "***Continue to ask, and God will give to you. Continue to search, and you will find. Continue to knock, and the door will open for you***" (Mathew 7:7 ICB). You might not get an immediate answer the first time but never stop asking and searching and knocking. Sometimes, a quiet moment of reflection can reveal insights about your calling that you might not have considered.

Your prayer might be as simple as this " ***Lord, please show me what you have called me to do with the life you have given me.***"

### Step 2. Self-Reflection:

Take a moment to explore the activities and experiences that light up your world and fill you with joy. What makes your heart sing and time fly by? These moments are like clues to unlocking your unique gifts and talents. For instance, imagine the feeling of being completely absorbed in painting or drawing, lost in the flow of creativity as your imagination comes to life on the canvas. Hours pass by effortlessly, and the end result brings a deep sense of satisfaction. This is more than just a hobby—it's a glimpse into your natural artistic abilities.

Grab a pen and paper and jot down your discoveries, starting with the activities that light you up the most. Let's uncover the treasures hidden within you!

## Step 3. Passions and Interests:

Dive into the world of your passions and interests. What topics or activities ignite a fire within you? Your interests hold the key to uncovering your hidden talents and potential. Perhaps you find yourself drawn to the adrenaline rush of sports, the wonders of science, the beauty of art, or the tranquility of nature. Maybe you feel a deep calling to stand up for what is right, or to be a voice for the voiceless.

Whatever stirs your soul and sparks your curiosity, take note of it. These passions are like signposts guiding you towards a path where your unique gifts can shine brightest.

## Step 4. Feedback from Others:

Seek feedback from family, mentors, and friends. What do they see as your strengths and talents? Their insights can provide valuable clues about your God-given gifts. It is very important to ask feedback not just from anybody but from people who truly love God and want to see you succeed in your God-given purpose.

Remember, your purpose is not a destination but a journey—a journey of growth, discovery, and alignment with the perfect will of God. As you unveil your purpose, let it be a beacon guiding you to a life of significance, where your unique gifts contribute to the flourishing of the Kingdom of God on earth.

# CHAPTER 4

## FACING THE GIANTS.

One of my son's favorite movies is "Facing the Giants". It's a captivating movie that follows the journey of a high school football coach, Grant Taylor, and his team as they confront seemingly insurmountable challenges both on and off the field. In six years of coaching, Coach Taylor has never led his Shiloh Eagles team to a winning season. Besides, he and his wife really want to have a baby, but it just hasn't happened yet. As the football season progresses, the team's lackluster performance begins to take its toll on the Coach. Despite his best efforts, the players seem demotivated and disheartened. However, Coach Taylor refuses to give up. With unwavering faith and determination, he encourages his team to give their all, regardless of the odds stacked against them.

As the team commits to a newfound spirit of excellence and perseverance, they begin to see remarkable changes both on and off the field. With faith as their cornerstone, they tackle challenges head-on and inspire the entire town with their resilience. Through heart-pounding victories and crushing defeats, Coach Taylor and his team learn valuable lessons about teamwork, dedication, and the power of faith to overcome adversity.

*In the end, they discover that true success isn't measured by wins and losses but by the strength of character and the courage to face life's giants with unwavering resolve.*

In the journey to fulfill your God given purpose, you will face adversity. It's important that you grasp that challenges are not obstacles meant to hinder you but stepping stones that lead to growth, resilience, and a deeper connection with God. Adversity, in various forms, is a universal experience. However, in the Kingdom perspective, it's not a signal to retreat but an invitation to advance with courage and faith.

In this chapter, I want to expose 3 main adversaries that you will encounter —the flesh, the world, and the devil. Each poses unique challenges that, when faced with resilience and faith, contribute to your growth :

## 1. The Flesh:

This adversary represents internal struggles, the inclinations, and desires within you that may lead you astray from God's purpose.

*Facing the flesh requires self-awareness, discipline, and a commitment to aligning your desires with the values of the Kingdom.*

Let's look at the example of Samson, a real-life superhero from the pages of the Bible! Imagine having muscles of steel and the power to take down armies single-handedly—that's Samson for you. But like all heroes, Samson had his weaknesses, and his biggest challenge wasn't fighting giant warriors—it was fighting his own desires.

Samson's strength came from his hair, which was a symbol of his special connection with God. But here's the twist: Samson fell head over heels for Delilah, a girl from a rival group called the Philistines. She was as cunning as she was beautiful, and she wanted to know Samson's secret.

Delilah nagged and nagged, trying to get Samson to spill the beans about his strength. And oh boy, did he fall for it! In a moment of weakness, he spilled the secret: his hair! As soon as Delilah cut it, Samson lost his super strength and got captured by the Philistines.

But here's the cool part: even in his lowest moment, Samson realized his mistake. He learned that putting his desires first instead of listening to God was a big no-no. And when he finally turned back to God, he got his strength back and took down the bad guys, proving that true strength comes from trusting in God, not just big muscles.

## 2. The World[1]:

The world, with its various influences and distractions, can present challenges to your journey. It may tempt you to conform to its standards rather than God's.

*Facing the world involves cultivating discernment and staying true to the Kingdom principles amid worldly pressures.*

Let's look at Daniel and his faithful friends, Shadrach, Meshach, and Abednego — a team of brave buddies who stuck together through thick and thin! They lived in a distant land ruled by a powerful king, where the pressure to fit in was stronger than ever. But these friends had something more precious than gold: their unwavering commitment to honor God, no matter what.

Their adventure began when they were plucked from their homes and whisked away to serve in the king's grand palace. But here's the catch: the king's palace wasn't exactly a place where people honored God. In fact, it was full of temptations and pressures to do things that went against Daniel and his friends' beliefs.

When the king served up fancy food that didn't align with their faith, Daniel and his friends stood their ground and asked for simpler fare instead. And guess what? They ended up healthier and stronger than everyone else!

But that was just the start. The king went on to build a giant golden statue and demanded that everyone bow down and worship it. But Daniel's friends? They said, "No way!" Even when faced with the threat of being thrown into a fiery

---

1    not the planet earth but the systems that govern the society we live in

furnace, they refused to betray their commitment to honor God.

And here's the best part: God was right there with them through it all. When they were tossed into the flames, they weren't harmed at all. God protected them because they stayed true to their beliefs, even in the face of danger.

## 3. The Devil:

*The devil is a cunning adversary, seeking to undermine your faith, sow doubt, and divert you from the Kingdom path.*

Recognizing and countering the tactics of the devil is essential for standing firm in the face of adversity.

Let's go back to the garden of Eden. The bible tells us that the serpent was more cunning than any other creature. With smooth words and clever tricks, he approached Eve and questioned God's command not to eat from the tree of the knowledge of good and evil. "***Did God really say you couldn't eat from any tree in the garden?***" he whispered, sowing seeds of doubt in Eve's mind.

Eve, innocent and curious, engaged in conversation with the serpent. He painted a picture of the forbidden fruit as something desirable and beneficial, promising that it would open her eyes and make her like God. Adam & Eve succumbed to temptation by eating of the forbidden fruit. The serpent, now revealed as the devil, had deceived them with his crafty words, leading them into disobedience and separation from God.

The temptation in the Garden of Eden serves as a cautionary tale, highlighting the cunning nature of the adversary. The devil is a master manipulator, twisting the truth and preying on our weaknesses to lead us astray. But we can learn from Adam and Eve's mistake by staying vigilant, guarding our hearts against the enemy's deceitful schemes, and trusting in God's guidance and truth.

*The devil is a master manipulator, twisting the truth and preying on our weaknesses to lead us astray.*

Facing these giants requires you to be equipped with the right weapons. Turn to the next page to discover The Kingdom Arsenal !

# TOOLS FOR CONFRONTING ADVERSITY

Just like a soldier or a football player preparing for battle or for a game need all sort of equipment to protect themselves and engage the adversary, so do you as a kingdom citizen.

*Picture a set of tools designed specifically for you, crafted to fortify your heart, mind, and spirit as you navigate the challenges of life.*

## Ephesian 6:10-18

*"Finally, be strong in the Lord and in his great power. Wear the full armor of God. Wear God's armor so that you can fight against the devil's evil tricks. Our fight is not against people on earth. We are fighting against the rulers and authorities and the powers of this world's darkness. We are fighting against the spiritual powers of evil in the heavenly world. That is why you need to get God's full armor. Then on the day of evil you will be able to stand strong. And when you have finished the whole fight, you will still be standing. So stand strong, with the belt of truth tied around your waist. And on your chest wear the protection of right living. And on your feet wear the Good News of peace to help you stand strong. And also use the shield of faith. With that you can stop all the burning arrows of the Evil One. Accept God's salvation to be your helmet. And take the sword of the Spirit—that sword is the teaching of God. Pray in the Spirit at all times. Pray with all kinds of prayers and ask for everything you need. To do this you must always be ready. Never give up. Always pray for all God's people.*

A soldier and a football player have physical pieces of protective equipment that they wear. They are real things you can see and feel. But for you, instead of actual concrete things to put on the body, your armor isn't something you can actually pick up. The pieces of your armor are attributes that God gives you to protect your mind, heart and spirit. Let discover them:

## 1. The Belt of Truth:

The belt of truth helps keep you grounded. In today's world, like never before, people make their own truth and live according to them. They go with whatever feels right or makes them feel good, but when you are a child of the King, the truth must come from God and His Word, not made-up opinions for what feels right in the moment.

## 2. The Breastplate of Righteousness:

As you face the giants, you will likely end up with some cuts and bruises on your arms and legs but those probably won't stop you from fighting. Nevertheless, very few soldiers can  survive a wound to their heart. That's why a breastplate is essential. It is the second piece that protects some very vital organs inside your body, including your heart. As citizens of the Kingdom of God, we should all be striving to live righteously. That means doing your best to do what is right and good according to God's Word and avoiding what the Bible says is evil. When we strive to live like this, we are protecting our spiritual hearts, just like a breastplate, from the damage that sin (living outside of the will of God) can inflict on our hearts.

### 3. The Good news of peace:

A battle won't go very well if you're just stuck in place. You've got to move forward. You certainly wouldn't wear flip flops for a race; that would make you unprepared to win.
Likewise, your feet can't be unprepared when you're fighting giants. According to the word of God, we must put on our feet the shoes that prepare us to tell the good news of peace. Our job as citizen of the kingdom of God is to share the good news of how Jesus came to save us from darkness.

### 4. The Shield of Faith:

Having the shield of faith, means having faith that God will stand against anything hurled your way. Negativity and lies will come into your life, but those fiery arrows get stopped in
their tracks when they are blocked with the shield of faith. Raise your shield of faith to deflect the arrows of doubt from the devil. Trust in God's promises and stand firm against the challenges presented by the world.

### 5. The Helmet of salvation:

Equally as important as protecting your heart in battle, a soldier or a football player absolutely must protect his head. Being confident that God has saved you and made you his child is the best
way to defend your mind from the lies and the challenges in life that these giants will attack you with.

### 6. The Sword of Truth:

All the above armor is worn or used for defensive purposes, to keep the bad things away. But the sixth and final piece listed in Ephesians is offensive. The sword of the Spirit which is the word of God. You

are protected with all the other pieces, but this one points you in the right direction. Knowing God's Word helps you attack the enemy. The devil knows God's Word is true, and when he hears it from your mouth, he doesn't like it! Using the truth of Scripture makes him back down. Having God's Word in our hearts on our lips is a tactic that can send the devil running in a hurry.

## Let the truth guide your decisions and actions.

Remember, as you confront adversity, you are not alone. The King walks with you, and His Kingdom Arsenal is at your disposal. Each challenge is an opportunity for growth, a moment to deepen your trust in God, and a step forward in your God-given purpose.

# CHAPTER 5

## CONQUERING THE FLESH

# UNDERSTANDING THE INTERNAL STRUGGLES

### Adversary: The Flesh

In this chapter, we'll delve into the internal battles we face—the desires, inclinations, and impulses that can divert us from God's plan.

The word of God paints a vivid picture of the war between the flesh and the Spirit. In Galatians 5:16-17, Paul highlights this internal struggle, emphasizing the need to walk by the Spirit and not gratify the desires of the flesh.

Do you ever feel like there's a war going on inside of you? Like there are two sides pulling you in different directions? Well, guess what? You're not alone. Even the strongest people have battles raging within them.

Think of it like this: Imagine there's a superhero version of you and a villain version of you. The superhero side wants to do what's right, be kind to others, and make good choices. But the villain side wants to do the opposite – be selfish, make bad choices, and sometimes even hurt others.

This is what Paul talks about in Galatians 5:16-17 (ICB) "*So, I tell you: Live by following the Spirit. Then you will not do what your sinful selves want. Our sinful selves want what is against the Spirit. The Spirit wants what is against our sinful selves. The two are against each other. So, you must not do just what you please*".

*It means that there's a constant battle between doing what's right and doing what's wrong.*

What does that mean for us? It means that there's a constant battle between doing what's right and doing what's wrong. Sometimes it's hard to know which voice to listen to – the one telling us to be kind and helpful or the one telling us to be selfish and mean.

## For kids your age, these battles might look like:

1. Peer Pressure: Feeling pressured to do things you know are wrong or make you uncomfortable, just to fit in with your friends.

2. Self-Doubt: Doubting yourself and your abilities, feeling like you're not good enough or that you'll never succeed.

3. Anger and Frustration: Getting angry easily or feeling frustrated when things don't go your way, even if you know it's not the right response.

4. Temptation: Being tempted to do things you know are wrong, like lying, cheating, or being mean to others, even though you know it's not right.

But here's the good news – you don't have to fight these battles alone. Just like a superhero has allies to help them defeat the villain, you have support too. You have family, friends, teachers, and a faith community who are there to help you make good choices and overcome those inner struggles.

*So, when you feel like there's a battle raging inside of you, remember that you have the power to choose which side wins.*

Choose kindness, choose love, and choose to be the superhero version of yourself. And with the help of your allies, you can conquer those inner battles and become the best version of yourself.

Remember, you're not alone in this fight. You've got what it takes to overcome those inner struggles and emerge victorious.

# PRACTICAL TIPS FOR VICTORY

- Recognizing Triggers: Identifying triggers is akin to deciphering a map. Know what situations, emotions, or environments tend to lead you toward negative behaviors or thoughts. Awareness is the first step toward victory.

- Mind Renewal: Engaging in activities that renew your mind is akin to reprogramming a computer. Reading uplifting books, listening to positive music, or practicing gratitude can contribute to rewiring your thought patterns.

- Accountability Partners: No warrior faces battles alone. Share your struggles with a trusted friend or mentor. Having someone to confide in provides support and accountability, turning the battle into a collective effort.

# CHAPTER 6

## NAVIGATING FRIENDSHIP AND PEER PRESSURE

# THE INFLUENCE OF THE WORLD

### Adversary: The World

This chapter will focus on the external challenges we face—the influences, values, and distractions that may lead us away from the Kingdom's principles.

Proverbs 13:20 serves as a guiding principle, emphasizing the impact of the company we keep: "***Walk with the wise and become wise, for a companion of fools suffers harm***." Additionally, 1 Corinthians 15:33 highlights the contagious nature of bad company, urging us to choose our friends wisely. "***Do not be so deceived and misled! Evil companionships (communion, associations) corrupt and deprave good manners and morals and character***."

So, what does that mean for us? It means that the people we surround ourselves with can have a big impact on our choices and who we become.

*If we hang out with friends who make good choices and encourage us to do the same, we're more likely to stay on the right path. But if we're always with friends who make bad choices, it can lead us down a dangerous road.*

## Let's break it down with some real-life examples:

1. Social Media Pressure: You might feel pressured to post certain things online or participate in trends that you're not comfortable with, just because everyone else is doing it.

2. Peer Influence on Schoolwork: Your friends might try to convince you to skip studying or cheat on a test, even though you know it's wrong.
3. Experimenting with Substances: Some kids might pressure you to try drugs, alcohol, or vaping, even though you know it's not safe or legal.
4. Bullying and Cliques: You might feel pressured to act a certain way or exclude others to fit in with a popular group, even if it goes against your values of kindness and inclusivity.

But guess what? You don't have to give in to peer pressure! You have the power to make your own choices and stand up for what you believe in. Here are some superhero strategies to help you navigate peer pressure like a pro:

# TIPS FOR CHOOSING POSITIVE FRIENDSHIPS

- Shared Values: Seek friends who share your values and encourage your spiritual growth. Building relationships with those who align with your Kingdom principles creates a supportive and uplifting environment.

- Healthy Boundaries: Friendship, like any relationship, requires boundaries. Establish and communicate healthy boundaries with friends to maintain a positive and supportive environment. This might involve open communication about your values and limits. Know what you stand for and don't be afraid to stick to your principles, even if it means going against the crowd.

- Speak Up: If you're feeling pressured to do something you know is wrong, don't be afraid to speak up and say no. Real friends will respect your decision.

- Seek Support: Don't be afraid to talk to a trusted adult – whether it's a parent, teacher, or counselor – if you're feeling overwhelmed by peer pressure.

Remember, you're not alone in this. With the wisdom of the Bible and the support of your allies, you can conquer peer pressure and stay true to yourself. You're a superhero in the making, and nothing can stop you from shining bright!

# CHAPTER 7

## OVERCOMING THE WEAPON OF FEAR

# UNMASKING THE TACTICS OF THE DEVIL

### Adversary: The Devil

This chapter will explore the subtle weapon the devil often employs against us—fear—and how we can overcome it.

*You see, fear is like a sneaky shadow that tries to hide in the corners of our minds, waiting to pounce when we least expect it.*

Imagine fear as a dark cloud hovering over your head, whispering scary thoughts into your ear. It's like a bully that tries to make you feel small and powerless. But here's the thing – fear is not your friend. It's not something that comes from God, who gives us strength, love, and a clear mind.

The bible abounds with assurances of overcoming fear. 2 Timothy 1:7 reminds us that "***God has not given us a spirit of fear but of power, love, and a sound mind***". Psalm 34:4 emphasizes seeking the Lord in times of fear, resulting in deliverance from all anxieties.

These verses provide a foundation for understanding the nature of fear and the divine resources available to conquer it.

So, what exactly is fear, and how does it sneak its way into our lives? Well, fear can come in many shapes and sizes, like:

1. Worry: Have you ever felt anxious or nervous about something, like a big test or a new experience? That's fear trying to make you doubt yourself and your abilities.
2. Doubt: Fear can make you second-guess yourself and your decisions. It can make you feel unsure and hesitant, like you're walking on shaky ground.
3. Scary Thoughts: Sometimes fear fills our minds with scary thoughts and what-ifs. It tries to make us imagine the worst-case scenarios, even if they're not likely to happen.
4. Physical Reactions: Fear can also show up in our bodies, making our hearts race, our palms sweat, and our stomachs churn. It's like our body's way of saying, "Hey, something's not right here!"

*We have the power to stand up to fear and chase it away with courage and faith.*

But here's the good news – fear doesn't have to control us! We have the power to stand up to fear and chase it away with courage and faith. Just like shining a light in a dark room, we can banish fear with the light of God's love and strength.

So, the next time you feel fear creeping in, remember that you are a brave and mighty warrior. With God by your side and a spirit of courage in your heart, you can conquer any fear and emerge victorious!

# STRATEGIES FOR VICTORY OVER FEAR

- Identifying Fear Triggers: Fear often has specific triggers. Identifying these triggers involves introspection and self-awareness. What situations, thoughts, or uncertainties tend to induce fear? Recognizing these triggers empowers you to face them head-on.

- Prayer and Meditation: Establishing a routine of prayer and meditation is akin to forging a shield against fear. Prayer connects you with the divine source of strength, and meditation allows for a stillness that calms the anxious mind.

- Positive Affirmations: Fear speaks lies. Counteract these lies with positive affirmations grounded in Scripture. Memorize verses that instill courage and repeat them as a tune in moments of fear.

# ACTIVITY OPERATION GIANT SLAYER: YOUR MISSION BEGINS

Welcome to "Operation Giant Slayer: Your Mission Begins"! Get ready to embark on a thrilling adventure filled with daring feats and epic victories, as you channel the courage and cunning of a legendary hero. Your mission? To confront the towering giants in your life and emerge as a true hero of the Kingdom.

**Let's dive in:**

1. **Identify Your Villains:**

Just like heroes face formidable foes, you too have your own adversaries—the giants that stand in your way. Is it the sneaky whispers of self-doubt, the pressure to fit in like a master strategist, or the looming shadow of fear? Write down your archenemies in the space provided below. It's time to expose them and take them down, in true hero fashion.

[List your personal villains here]

_____

_____

2. **Size Up Your Targets:**

Now, let's analyze these villains like a hero assesses their enemies. Where do they come from? How do they make you feel? What tricks do they use to trap you? Take a moment to ponder these questions and jot down your findings. Remember, knowing your enemy is the key to outsmarting them.

[Analyze your targets here]

_____

_____

_____

_____

3. **Unleash Your Secret Weapons:**

Just like heroes have their arsenal, you too have powerful tools at your disposal to defeat your adversaries. Here are your secret weapons:

- Faith: Trust in the power of the Almighty, knowing that He is your ultimate ally.

- Courage: Embrace your inner hero and face your fears head-on, armed with bravery and determination.

- Preparation: Equip yourself with knowledge and resilience, ready to tackle any challenge that comes your way.

Which of these secret weapons will you wield on your mission? Highlight your choice and let it guide you to victory.

___

___

___

___

4. **Execute Your Mission:**

It's time to put your training into action, Agent. Use the space below to sketch, write, or craft your epic mission to slay your giants. Will you draw yourself in a fierce showdown with your villains, write a gripping tale of triumph, or create a top-secret dossier detailing your strategy? The choice is yours.

[Execute your mission here]

___

___

___

___

5. **Declare Your Triumph:**

As heroes triumph over their adversaries, so too shall you emerge victorious over your giants. Write a bold declaration of victory, affirming your courage, resilience, and unwavering determination to conquer your foes. This is your moment of triumph, Agent.

[Declare your triumph here]

_____

_____

_____

_____

Congratulations, young agent! You've embarked on a mission of epic proportions, armed with courage, faith, and an indomitable spirit. Keep this activity close as a reminder of your strength and resolve. Remember, with God on your side, you can overcome any challenge and emerge as a true hero of the Kingdom.

Now, go forth and conquer your giants with the bravery and determination of a true hero. The world awaits your heroic deeds!

With excitement and God's blessings.

# CHAPTER 8

## DEEPENING CONNECTIONS THROUGH PRAYER AND SPIRITUAL DISCIPLINE

# THE POWER OF INTENTIONAL CONNECTION

In the beginning of this book, we went through the story of the father and his two sons to highlight the fact that like a father, God wants to have a close relationship with you as His child. Prayer and spiritual disciplines (studying the Bible, praying, and fasting) are the bedrock of our relationship with God. Having a strong and vibrant connection with God our King is important to successfully fulfill our purpose.

You see, just like superheroes have their secret training routines to hone their powers, we have our own supercharged practices to strengthen our spirits.

In the Bible, it talks about the importance of spending time in prayer and nurturing our spiritual selves. Jesus Himself showed us the way by often withdrawing to solitary places to pray (Luke 5:16), and He taught us about the power of private prayer, saying, "***But when you pray, go into your room, close the door and pray to your Father, who is unseen. Then your father, who sees what is done in secret, will reward you.***" (Matthew 6:6)

So, why are prayer and spiritual disciplines so important for us? Well, let's break it down:

1. Connection with God: Just like chatting with your best friend, prayer is your direct line to God. It's where you can share your joys, worries, and dreams with Him and feel His love surrounding you.

2. Strength for the Journey: Life can be like a rollercoaster ride with ups and downs. But when you take time to pray and meditate on God's word regularly, you build up your inner strength to face whatever comes your way.

3. Finding Peace: In the hustle and bustle of everyday life, it's easy to feel overwhelmed and stressed out. But when you carve out quiet moments for prayer and reflection, you invite peace into your heart and mind.

4. Growing Closer to God: Just like watering a plant, spiritual disciplines like reading the Bible, worshiping, and serving others help you grow closer to God and deepen your relationship with Him.

Think of prayer and studying the word of God as your secret superpowers. They might not give you the ability to fly or shoot lasers from your eyes, but they give you something even better – the power to conquer challenges, spread love, and shine bright in a dark world.

So, start incorporating prayer and spiritual disciplines into your life by following these guidelines:

- Prayer as Conversation: Prayer is more than a monologue; it's a dialogue with God our King. Cultivate a conversational style of prayer, pouring out your heart, and allowing space to listen for God's voice. Create a personalized prayer journal to document your conversations with Him. Include prayers, reflections, and insights gained during your time alone with the King.

- Scripture Meditation: Immerse yourself in the richness of the bible. Meditating on God's Word allows His truth to take root in your heart, shaping your thoughts and actions.

- Fasting Integrate fasting into your spiritual routine. This practice, combined with prayer, deepens your awareness of God's presence, and sharpens your spiritual focus.

- Community Connection: Engage in communal spiritual practices. Participate in group prayer, Bible studies, and church gatherings to strengthen your connection with both God and fellow believers.

- Weekly Spiritual Audit: Conduct a weekly spiritual audit, assessing your engagement with prayer and other disciplines. Celebrate progress, identify areas for growth, and recalibrate your spiritual routine as needed.

# CHAPTER 9

**EMPOWERED TO IMPACT**

# UNLEASHING YOUR KINGDOM INFLUENCE

As we come to the end of this book, I hope you understand who you are as a person and that you are here on earth for a specific purpose that God took the time to craft just for you. I strongly believe that It's your time to unleash all the potential that is within you and make a positive impact on the world around you.

In the Bible, Jesus tells us, "***You are the salt of the earth... You are the light of the world... Let your light shine before others, that they may see your good deeds and glorify your Father in heaven***." (Matthew 5:13-16) What does that mean? It means that you have the power to make a difference, to bring flavor and brightness to the world, just like salt and light do.

Let's go back to our three faith heroes we saw in previous chapter, Dorcas, Corrie Ten Boom and Nick:

Dorcas: used her sewing skills to make clothes for those in need. She showed love and compassion to others through her actions, making a positive impact in her community.

Corrie and her family helped many Jewish people escape the Nazis by hiding them in their home. Despite facing great danger, Corrie's faith and courage inspired hope in others and saved countless lives.

Nick didn't let his physical condition stop him from making a difference. He travels the world sharing his story of faith and resilience, encouraging others to overcome their challenges and find hope in God.

These heroes weren't afraid to let their light shine bright, and neither should you! Here are some superhero tips for shining bright in the world:

# TOOLS FOR IMPACTFUL LIVING

- Identifying God-Given Gifts: Reflect on your unique gifts and talents you already identified with your gift compass. Give thanks to God for entrusting you with these gifts for the benefits of others.

- Service and Compassion: Embrace a lifestyle of service and compassion. Acts of kindness, both big and small, reflect the love of Christ and contribute to positive change in your community.

- Advocacy and Social Justice: Stand up for justice and equality. Advocating for those who are marginalized or oppressed aligns with the Kingdom principles of love and justice.

# CREATING A RIPPLE EFFECT

- Community Projects: Initiate or participate in community projects that address specific needs. Whether it's a food drive, environmental initiative, or educational program, your actions can create a ripple effect of positive change.

- Amplifying Voices: Use your platform to amplify the voices of the marginalized. Advocate for equal opportunities in your spheres of influence.

- Prayer for Impact: Anchor your efforts in prayer. Pray for wisdom, discernment, and divine guidance as you navigate the path of making a positive impact in your community.

Before closing the book, I want to make sure you and I are on the same side, that we are both part of God's family. If you've already invited Jesus in your life and follow him, that is very great. But if you are not sure or have never invited him in your life, I want you to join God's family now. Jesus' friend John, tells us in one of his messages:

*There was a man named John who was sent by God. He came to tell people about the Light. Through him all people could hear about the Light and believe. John was not the Light, but he came to tell people about the Light. The true Light was coming into the world. The true Light gives light to all. The Word was in the world. The world was made through him, but the world did not know him. He came to the world that was his own. But his own people did not accept him. But some people did accept him. They believed in him. To them he gave the right to become children of God. They did not become his children in the human way. They were not born because of the desire or wish of some man. They were born of God.*
**(John 1:6-13 ICB)**

John is explaining that even though Jesus is the Life and Light that men need, some will choose to walk out on him and remain in darkness. But to those who will welcome him for who he is, The Word of God, the true Light that came into the world to rescue us from the power of darkness, they receive the privilege, the right to become children of God. When I say welcome him, it means you believe him and trust him for all he is and all he has done and will do with all your heart, mind and strength.

Through this message, understand that becoming a member of God's family does not happen the same way you were born to your mom and dad. You just need to receive Jesus in your heart and God himself will make sure you become part of his family. God wants a big family and there is room for everyone who wants to be part of it. I encourage you to respond to his invitation and join us today!

Take one moment and say this prayer out loud and do this to the best of your knowledge and understanding:

***Dear Lord Jesus, I believe you are the Word of God and the light of the world. Thank you that you have come into this world to rescue me from the power of darkness. I believe you and I invite you today to come into my heart and life. I want to trust and follow You as my Lord and Savior forever and ever. In Your Name I pray. Amen!***

After saying this prayer, nothing happens to you physically. In your body you have not felt any change. But in the spirit world, which is invisible to your physical eyes, the place where Jesus and the angels dwell, something beautiful has happened. You have been carried with great power and joy from darkness to Light. Remember we saw with John that Jesus is Light. So, you have been carried to where he is. You are officially a child of God !

This calls for a celebration (write this date in your journal).

www.ingramcontent.com/pod-product-compliance
Lightning Source LLC
LaVergne TN
LVHW051057100526
838202LV00087BA/6560